CHRISTIANITY AND SEX

IVP Series in Contemporary Christian Thought

Christianity and Philosophy by Dr. Arthur F. Holmes, Director of Philosophy, Wheaton College

Emil Brunner: An Introduction to the Man and His Thought by Dr. Paul K. Jewett, Associate Professor of Systematic Theology, Fuller Theological Seminary

Christianity and Aesthetics by Dr. Clyde S. Kilby, Professor and Chairman, Department of English, Wheaton College

An Interpretation of Karl Barth by Dr. Kenneth S. Kantzer, Professor of Bible, Chairman of the Division of Bible and Philosophy, Wheaton College

Jesus Christ and History by Dr. George Eldon Ladd, Professor of Biblical Theology, Fuller Theological Seminary

Christianity
and
Sex
by

Stuart Barton Babbage

Professor Elect of Christian Apologetics, Columbia Theological Seminary; Principal, Ridley College, Melbourne; Formerly, Dean, St. Andrew's Cathedral, Sydney, and St. Paul's Cathedral, Melbourne

Inter-Varsity Press   *Chicago 10*

Library of Congress catalog card number: 63–8554

Cover design by Jack Sidebotham

Printed in the United States of America

Preface

STUDENTS OF THE BIBLE find it significant that sexuality appears in the opening pages of the book of Genesis. God's creation of man in the divine image is closely related to human existence in male and female forms.

God created man in his own image . . . male and female he created them.

. . . the Lord God said, "It is not good that the man should be alone; I will make him a helper fit for him."

Therefore a man . . . cleaves to his wife, and they become one flesh.

—Genesis 1:27; 2:18, 24

From the very beginning of Scripture, the marriage relationship is blessed by God as reflecting in part the image of the Creator.

And God blessed them, and God said to them, "Be fruitful and multiply, and fill the earth and subdue it; and have dominion. . . ."

—Genesis 1:28

Man and woman were intended to be one—created in His image in holiness, in creativeness, and in ability to rule under God over all creation.

As the unity of man and woman at its best reflects the image of God, so disorders of sex and marriage mirror most startlingly the far-reaching corruption of man. Sex and marriage can become ends in themselves, and thus idolatry. Sex can become diseased, degraded, destructive; it can be exploited and deified. Yet man and marriage are both renewable through redemption—so much so that the Bible uses this most intimate of personal relationships as an analogy of the bond between God and His people, Christ and His Church.

No area outside the God-man relationship is so vital or so decisive for men and women as that of sex. Probably no aspect of human life is more complex. For these reasons we need to understand—in order to direct—this great instinctive drive, with its vast potentialities for good or ill.

This monograph does not pretend to be an exhaustive treatment of sex; it is not a complete guide to courtship and marriage. It is a statement of the biblical view of sex. *Christianity and Sex* meets an urgent need for a clear presentation of God's viewpoint as we appraise and reappraise our often contradictory values and actions in this important area.

Contents

I. Views of the Human Body

No DISCRIMINATING READER of the plays of Bernard Shaw can fail to detect, underlying all his work, a strange contempt for the human body. This aversion is partly the expression of an exaggerated intellectualism, but it is more than that. It is a Manichean hatred for the physical organism as such. (Manicheism is the ancient heresy that matter is evil, and that therefore the body is evil.)

In *Back to Methusaleh* "the Ancients" look forward to discarding their bodies as Shaw believes they once discarded their tails. In Act III of *Man and Superman* Shaw writes: "This earth is a nursery in which men and women play at being heroes and heroines, saints and sinners, but they are dragged down from their fool's paradise by their bodies." In the life of the world to come, Shaw declares, "you escape this tyranny of the flesh . . . you are not an animal at all; you are a ghost, an appearance, an illusion, a convention, deathless, ageless, in a word, bodiless."

This view is one which many Christians find congenial and strangely attractive. It is incompatible with the traditional teaching of the Bible. The Christian believes that for fullness of life man needs a body, not only in this life but also in the life to come. That is why, in the Apostles' Creed, he affirms his belief "in the resurrection of the body" as well as in "the life everlasting."

Bernard Shaw, in his Manichean aversion to and contempt for the body, is not unique. The same note of underlying revulsion is to be found in the works of T. E. Lawrence. This accounts for the sketches in *The Seven Pillars of Wisdom* in which he apparently delights in ridiculing and mocking his absurd little self. He has a feeling of disgust for the humiliating weakness, the ludicrous absurdity of his body. This feeling was to manifest itself in self-inflicted masochism on the one hand and insatiable sadism on the other.

Manicheism has an ancient lineage. Manichean overtones exist in much Platonic thought. According to Greek thought, the body is a prison from which the soul is released only by death. "For the body is a source of endless trouble to us by reason of the mere requirement of food; and is liable also to diseases which overtake us and impede us in the search after true being: it fills us full of loves, and lusts, and fears, and fancies of all kinds, and endless foolery, and, in fact, as men say, takes away from us the power of thinking at all. Whence come wars, and fightings, and factions? Whence but from the body and lusts of the body?" So Plato reports Socrates in the *Phaedo*.[1] In the life to come, Socrates continues, we shall have "got rid of the foolishness of the body"; then, "we shall be pure and hold converse with the pure, and know of ourselves the clear light everywhere which is no other than the light of truth."

Plato uses a variety of ingenious analogies to illustrate the nature of man's present bondage. There is the

[1] 65c-66a.

analogy of the charioteer and the winged horses. One horse is of noble origin, the other ignoble; the one is striving continually to mount to the region of the heavens, and to look upon the images of the divine beauty and wisdom that are proper to its nature; the other is ever dragging the chariot down to the earth and to earthly delights. The wise man, according to Plato, subjugates the body to the soul; he represses the "beast" within him. He withdraws "from the body as far as the conditions of life allow"; he makes life "one long study for death." [2]

Again, there is the analogy of the chains by which a man is bound as a prisoner in a cave, the chains being man's animal nature. In childhood and youth, Plato declares, the activity of reason is checked by the imperious and insistent demands of appetite. If reason is reinforced by education, progress is possible; but often the fetters of the soul, instead of being weakened and broken, are riveted even more firmly by repeated acts of self-indulgence.[3]

The Neo-Platonist Plotinus, according to his contemporaries, seemed ashamed of his body, and thanked God that he had not been created with an immortal body.[4]

The Biblical View of the Body

It needs to be said at once that these views are unbiblical. The Bible affirms that when God made man,

[2] *Phaedo*, 65-67; *Phaedrus*, 250.
[3] *Timaeus*, 43a.
[4] Porphyry, *Life of Plotinus*.

He made him male and female, and that, having made him, He said that he was "very good" (Genesis 1:31). No Christian, then, can subscribe to the view that man's body is a "tomb"; on the contrary, he must insist with the Apostle Paul that man's body is a "temple" (I Corinthians 6:19). The body of man is not something humiliating, almost disgusting, but something holy; not an impediment and hindrance to the life of man, but an indispensable instrument for the expression of the personality. That is why the Christian does not look forward in the life to come to a state of disembodied existence but to the possession of a body, a body no longer subject to weakness and infirmity, but a transfigured body of resplendent glory unhampered by sin and sickness (I Corinthians 15:35 ff).

The adoption of unbiblical views about the body are the result of an unfortunate confusion between "the body" and "the flesh." In biblical terminology "the flesh" refers to man's sinful nature. (The Apostle enumerates what he means by "the works of the flesh" in Galatians 5:19 ff.) Although "the body," created by God from "the dust of the ground," can be misused in the service of sin, it is not in itself sinful. As Luther points out, our Lord was sinless even though He had a body, and the devil is sinful even though he is without a body. Luther adds that it was the devil who spoiled the beautiful sex instinct which God made, so that pure love was changed into lust, childbirth became painful, and nakedness was associated with shame.[5] But the

[5] Olavi Lahteenmaki, *Sexus und Ehe bei Luther,* pp. 48-49.

body itself is not sinful, though it can become the instrument of sin and the slave of sin.

A careful distinction is made in the pages of the New Testament between "the flesh" and "the body." "Let not sin therefore reign in your mortal body," writes St. Paul, "neither yield ye your members as instruments of unrighteousness unto sin" (Romans 6:12, 13). For sin to have dominion is an illegitimate usurpation of the crown rights of the Redeemer. Paul indicates with careful exactitude the locus of sin: it is "the flesh"—that is, in biblical usage, the unsanctified nature of fallen man—which is sinful and not "the body." "I know that in me," he writes, "that is, in my flesh, dwelleth no good thing" (Romans 7:18). That is why the Christian needs to learn to walk in the Spirit so that he will not fulfill "the lusts of the flesh," of human nature deprived of the Spirit of God (Galatians 5:16).

Early Christian Asceticism

In the first centuries of the Christian era, the Gnostics adopted the pagan view that the body itself is evil. Satornilus branded marriage and the begetting of children as the work of Satan. Marcion insisted on either celibacy, or continence within marriage, as obligatory for all Christians. In the apocryphal *Acts of John*, the Apostle, invited to a wedding, explains to the bridal pair that the conjugal act is a crime and a sin. Likewise, in the *Acts of Paul*, there is an exaggerated exaltation of virginity and celibacy in a series of fresh beatitudes:

[5

Blessed are they that keep the flesh chaste . . .
Blessed are they that abstain . . .
Blessed are they that have renounced the world . . .
Blessed are they that possess their wives as though they
  had them not . . .
Blessed are the bodies of virgins . . .

The embarrassed repudiation of the body was responsible for a denigration of sex, which resulted both
in the growth of antinomianism and in the development of asceticism. An antinomian is one who shows
his freedom from the law, and his contempt for the
body, by living without moral scruple a life of licence.
An ascetic is one who shows his contempt for the body
by the practice of self-flagellation and cruel mortifica-
tion. The consequence of these two tendencies was
licentiousness and libertarianism on the one hand and
barbarous severity on the other.

The ascetics went to extraordinary lengths in a vain
attempt to escape from what the Apostle John calls "the
lust of the flesh and the lust of the eyes" (I John 2:16).
Jerome, who did so much to promote the growth of
asceticism in the West, took refuge in the solitude of the
desert to escape the disturbing and corrupting presence
of women. Alone in his cell, he found himself tormented
by lascivious dreams of dancing women, and this puz-
zled him the more, since his emaciated limbs were
numb with cold.

The so-called "pillar saints" were the most bizarre
expression of the ascetic spirit. In his poem *Saint
Simeon Stylites*, Tennyson describes the hideous mis-
eries of this ascetic who remained on the top of a pillar,

exposed to wind and weather, for over thirty years.

Origen, that brilliant and erratic genius, also embraced asceticism. Like his predecessor Pantaenus, he boldly called himself a Christian Gnostic. In a rash moment of literalistic zeal, which later he was bitterly to regret, he made himself an eunuch for the kingdom of heaven's sake (Matthew 18:8-9; 19:12).

Platonism and Gnosticism were responsible for an unhappy legacy of ascetic exaggeration in the life of the Church: an asceticism which manifested itself in an undue exaltation of celibacy on the one hand and an unbiblical depreciation of marriage on the other. John of Damascus, who collected sayings from the patristic fathers, quotes such observations as: "A woman is an evil," and "A beautiful woman is a whited sepulchre."

In Augustine the process reached its logical conclusion in the assertion that the act of physical intercourse cannot be separated from the lust of concupiscence. Augustine was chiefly responsible for the disastrous identification of sexuality with sin, and for the teaching that a peculiar taint attaches to the process of human reproduction. There is a strain of morbidity verging on the pathological in the thought of the celebrated Bishop of Hippo: he deplores the fact that God ever created sex and is embarrassed by the fact that He ordained it as the means of human reproduction. Augustine teaches that the processes of conception and birth are unseemly, unclean, shameful, and a hindrance to the holy life.

In the Cathari the aversion to sex takes an even more

[7

extreme and eccentric form. In their morbid and obsessional fear of sex they refused to eat anything associated with sex: eggs, cheese, butter, or milk.

In the Middle Ages the legislative enactments of the Roman Church reflected contemporary views about the impropriety of sex. They were designed to regulate and restrict sexual activity. On five days out of seven sexual abstinence was solemnly enjoined: on Thursdays, in memory of the arrest of our Lord; on Fridays, in commemoration of His death; on Saturdays, in honor of the blessed Virgin; on Sundays, in honor of the sacred departed.

With the reformers a more wholesome and refreshing note returns. The reformers insist that marriage is both a useful and enjoyable gift of God. Marriage is a divine ordinance; nevertheless, because of sin, it needs to be sanctified by the redemptive word of the gospel of Christ. You cannot sanctify sex by abstinence, Luther argues, nor can you sanctify marriage by making it a sacrament. Both can be sanctified only by God's grace. To teach that abstinence from sex is in itself meritorious is to advocate a kind of salvation "by works." To teach that marriage is a sacrament implies that there is a special kind of guilt inherent in the marriage relationship, and that particular rites of the Church are needed to free a couple from guilt. But man's alienation from God is due not to his nature but to his sin, and there is no more sin in sex than in any other aspect of man's life. It has been truly observed: "To think that the saying of prayers, or the refraining from sexual activity, could in themselves be agents of salvation was to misunderstand the total and organic nature of man's sin—sin being man's alienation from God and from what God intended him to be." [6]

II. The Biblical Presentation of Sex

IT IS TIME to leave this study of aberrations and exaggerations that disfigured the life of the patristic and medieval Church, distorting the biblical view of the body and the sex instinct. Following the example of the reformers themselves, we turn to an examination of biblical testimony on the subject of sex.

When God created man He created him male and female (Genesis 1:27). As a result of the creative activity of God, man exists in a state of sexual differentiation. His bisexuality is not only for the purpose of reproduction, but also for the sake of companionship: "And the Lord God said: It is not good that man should be alone; I will make a help mate for him" or, "a helper fit for him" (Genesis 2:18). God's work in creating Eve is recorded in picturesque language: "And the Lord God caused a deep sleep to fall upon Adam, and he slept:

[6] Seward Hiltner, Sex and the Christian Life (New York: Association Press, 1957), p. 60. Quoted by permission.

[9

and he took one of his ribs, and closed up the flesh instead thereof; and the rib, which the Lord God had taken from man, made he a woman, and brought her unto the man" (Genesis 2:21-22). Peter Lombard makes the ingenious comment: "Eve was not taken from the feet of Adam to be his slave, nor from his head to be his ruler, but from his side to be his beloved partner."

God, says the Psalmist, "setteth the solitary in families" (Psalm 68:6). Of each of the successive works of creation it is said that God saw that it was "good"; of the fact that man was alone, without a sexual counterpart as other creatures, God said: "It is not good." Knowing that it was not good for man to be alone, God delivered him from solitariness by giving him a wife, and in giving him a wife, He gave him a companion.

The Unitive Purpose of Sex

The relationship intended and established by God is one of mutual interdependence: neither the man without the woman nor the woman without the man. In the most literal sense, the man is made for the woman and the woman is made for the man. It is only when a man leaves his father and his mother, and cleaves unto his wife, and they become one flesh, that he discovers the secret of his manhood; in like manner, it is only when a woman leaves her father and her mother, and cleaves to her husband, and they become one flesh, that she discovers the secret of her womanhood. When a man learns "to know" his wife, he learns to know himself. In

10]

the experience of sexual intercourse, he not only pene-
trates the mystery of sex; he also discovers the secret of
his own being. This self-discovery marks his initiation
into manhood: in finding what he calls (more truly
than he knows) his "other half," or more generously,
his "better half," he finds himself.

In the gracious economy of God, the gift of sexuality .
is for purposes both unitive and procreative. In the experience of physical intercourse a man and a woman
become, in a sense both psychic and physical, "one
flesh" (Mark 10:8). The act of physical intercourse is
an act of supreme self-giving, of glad abandon; that is
why it properly marks the culmination and climax of
true love. A man in the act of intercourse gives himself
in total and joyous surrender to the woman he loves,
and the woman in like manner gives herself to the man.
It is the fact of surrender, of self-giving, that makes the
experience of intercourse, in the true sense of the word,
a sacramental thing. In the providence of God the physical act becomes a vehicle for the expression of feelings
too deep for words: the outward and visible sign of an
inward and spiritual grace. The act of intercourse is
more than a physical experience; it is also a profound
and deeply moving emotional experience—one that involves both partners in the totality of their being. In the
experience of intercourse a unity is consummated and
established, a unity in which they become "one flesh,"
and throughout life, that unity is renewed and sustained
by repeated acts of intercourse. This unitive act is sym-
bolic, expressive of an existing spiritual reality, and of
the fact that this man and this woman who are "one

[11

flesh" are one also in heart and mind. That is why the experience of intercourse is rightly regarded as properly limited to the marriage relationship: to those who, before God and the world, have publicly pledged their troth, each to the other, in a relationship which is declared to be not only exclusive but also permanent and binding.

The Degradation of Sex

Promiscuity is the degradation of love: it divorces the physical act from the context of love in which alone it finds its sanctity and meaning, thus evacuating the physical act of moral and spiritual significance. "Marriage," says the writer of the Epistle to the Hebrews, "is honorable in all, and the bed undefiled: but whoremongers and adulterers God will judge" (13:4). Lust, in contrast to love, is always exploitive, always selfish: it desecrates sex because it divorces the physical act from the context of love. It also involves the violation of personality. It treats another human being not as an end but as a means—a means for the gratification of fleeting lust.

One of the problems of our contemporary society is that the experience of love is so often made synonymous with the act of copulation. Consequently, that which is holy and sublime is degraded to the level of the animal and the genital. The outlook of the natural man is captured by T. S. Eliot in *Sweeney Agonistes*, in which the mystery of life is reduced to:

Birth, and copulation, and death,
That's all the facts when you come to brass tacks;
Birth, and copulation, and death.

Man indeed is made from "the dust of the ground." He shares with the rest of the animal creation a nervous and sensory system, but he is not simply an animal organism. He is also a moral and responsible being, made in "the image of God," and thereby capable, in a way which an animal is not, of self-transcendence. That is why a man can never be content with an animal existence—a life lived at the animal and the genital level. The man who attempts to live at the animal level makes "a beast of himself," and the beastliness of man, as M. V. C. Jeffreys points out, is always something quite different from the naturalness of the beast.[7] Life at the animal level contradicts the destiny which God intended for man. G. K. Chesterton once remarked:

If I wish to dissuade a man from drinking his tenth whisky and soda, I slap him on the back and say, "Be a man!" No one who wished to dissuade a crocodile from eating its tenth explorer would slap it on the back and say, "Be a crocodile!"

A crocodile cannot help being itself and obeying the law of its own carnivorous nature; but it is man's nature ever to be dissatisfied with "nature." As he is endowed with a higher dignity than any animal, so he is intended to live on a higher level of existence, as he hopes to enjoy a nobler destiny. That is why a man degrades

[7] *Glaucon* (London: Sir Isaac Pitman and Sons, Ltd., 1955), p. 5.

himself when he lives at the level of the instinctive and the sensual. God meant him to live a life characterized by moral responsibility and self-determination.

A man and a woman, in the intimate experience of intercourse, are made "one flesh." The natural man ignores this fact. The Apostle Paul asks the indignant question: "What? Know ye not that he which is joined to an harlot is one body? for two, saith he, shall be one flesh" (I Corinthians 6:16). Sexual immorality, he says, is not something external; it is an offense against a man's own body. That is why he adds the emphatic exhortation: "Flee fornication." Concerning this temptation there is to be no dallying and no delay: the man tempted to fornication is not to argue, but like Joseph, to flee. (Cf. Genesis 39:7 ff.)

The biblical phrase *one flesh* implies a union of a radical kind, a union which has been described by Derrick Bailey as organic and not simply arithmetical. It is not a sentimental union but a union of the utmost seriousness—a union which involves, at the deepest level, the confrontation and encounter of a man and a woman in an experience which is decisive and irrevocable.

The Procreative Purpose of Sex

"God," according to the biblical revelation, "created man in his own image, in the image of God created he him; male and female created he them. And God blessed them, and God said unto them, Be fruitful, and multiply, and replenish the earth, and subdue it"

14]

(Genesis 1:27-28). In the act of physical intercourse a man and a woman express the unity which binds them; attached to the exquisite ecstasy of the sexual experience is an added gift—the gift of being able to procreate. God permits man to share in the joyous task of creation. As God created man in His own image, so He permits man to create children in his own image. There is no higher privilege, no greater responsibility, than that of parenthood. The Christian man gladly acknowledges that "children are an heritage of the Lord," and that "the fruit of the womb are his reward" (Psalm 127:3). Consequently, the Christian man will pray earnestly that, having been put in trust with this gift, which is both a blessing and a burden, he may bring up the children who are the fruit of his loins "in the nurture and admonition of the Lord" (Ephesians 6:4).

The Modern Exploitation of Sex

No one can ignore the fact that sin has invaded the sanctum of sex, and that the gift of God, intended for the delight of man and the perpetuation of the race, has become an instrument of self-indulgence. As a consequence of the fall, God's good gift has been perverted from its true end and, in the life of sinful man, has become perplexing, destructive, and explosive.

C. S. Lewis has some pertinent observations to make. In his vivid epigrammatic way, he writes:

You can get a large audience together for a strip-tease act —that is, to watch a girl undress on the stage. Now suppose

[15

you came to a country where you could fill a theatre by simply bringing a covered plate on the stage and then slowly lifting the cover so as to let everyone see, just before the lights went out, that it contained a mutton chop or a bit of bacon, would you not think that in that country something had gone wrong with its appetite for food? And would not any one who had grown up in a different world think there was something equally queer about the state of the sex instinct among us?

He proceeds to demolish the specious arguments which are advanced to explain, and thereby to extenuate, the state of our sexual morality. Some say that sex is a mess because it has been hushed up ("But for the last twenty years it has not been hushed up. It has been chattered about all day long. Yet it is still in a mess."); that sex is nothing to be ashamed of ("There is nothing to be ashamed of in enjoying your food: there would be everything to be ashamed of if half the world made food the main interest of their lives and spent their time looking at pictures of food and dribbling and smacking their lips."); that sex is "natural" and "normal," and that those who repress their desires are perverse and abnormal ("Poster after poster, film after film, novel after novel, associate the idea of sexual indulgence with the ideas of health, normality, youth, frankness . . . Now this association is a lie . . . Surrender to all our desires obviously leads to impotence, disease, jealousies, lies, concealment, and everything that is the reverse of health, good humour, and frankness."); and finally, the convenient lie that sex "repression" is dangerous

16]

and that Christian chastity is impossible.[8] The claims and assertions that are so confidently made by the defenders of behavioristic psychology are not only false but wicked, and it is C. S. Lewis' supreme achievement that he has demonstrated this fact with cogency and wit.

In another place C. S. Lewis points out that practically the whole of the Christian faith can be deduced from two facts, one of which is that men make coarse jokes. The natural man has a compulsive interest in obscenity.

The coarse joke proclaims that we have here an animal which finds its own animality either objectionable or funny. Unless there had been a quarrel between the spirit and the organism I do not see how this could be: it is the very mark of the two not being "at home" together. But it is very difficult to imagine such a state of affairs as original—to suppose a creature which from the very first was half shocked and half tickled to death at the mere fact of being the creature it is. I do not perceive that dogs see anything funny about being dogs: I suspect that angels see nothing funny about being angels.[9]

But this is precisely man's predicament: he finds his sexuality at one and the same time embarrassing and amusing. His jokes are a smoke screen behind which he seeks to hide his feeling of self-consciousness and his sense of shame. There is, he feels, something incongru-

[8] *Mere Christianity* (New York: The Macmillan Co., 1952), pp. 76 ff. Quoted by permission.
[9] *Miracles* (New York: The Macmillan Co., 1947), p. 154. Quoted by permission.

[17

ous about the fact that a being capable of such pretentious claims reproduces itself in the way which it does. What this indicates is a deep schism within the life of man: an inner disharmony between the desires of the flesh and the aspirations of the mind (Romans 7:22-23). From this fact alone, C. S. Lewis argues, we might well deduce the fact of the fall.

Man is a fallen creature, and it is his inability to resolve his inner conflict that tempts him to seek an unreal solution in the barrenness of a self-stultifying asceticism or the degradation of a dreary sensuality. The problem of sex, however, can be solved neither by the desperate expedient of forced and frantic repression (even when carried to the extremity of castration), nor by the pursuit of unrestrained visceral emotion; the problem of sex can only be solved in the context of saving faith. The Christian accepts God's gift of sex without embarrassment and without shame, and relying on God's redemptive mercy, dedicates it to God's glory. "For everything created by God is good, and nothing is to be rejected if it is received with thanksgiving; for then it is consecrated by the word of God and prayer" (I Timothy 4:4, RSV).

The Pagan Deification of Sex

For the Christian, sex is neither a subject for jesting obscenity, nor an object for superstitious deification. Walt Whitman, like Schopenhauer before him, regarded sex as both the compendium of all meaning and the quintessence of reality. Whitman wrote:

18]

Sex contains all bodies, souls,
Meanings, proofs, purities, delicacies, results, promulgations,
Songs, commands, health, pride, the maternal mystery;
The seminal milk,
All hopes, benefactions, bestowals, all the passions, loves,
  beauties, delights of the earth,
All the governments, judges, gods, follow'd persons of the
  earth,
These are contain'd in sex as parts of itself and justification
  of itself.

This panegyric in praise of sex might even leave a Freudian breathless. There is something ironic in the fact that Whitman, whose own sex life was notoriously disordered and perverse, is the one who sings the praises of the sexual experience as the supreme revelation of life.

According to the preacher of Ecclesiastes, there is nothing new under the sun (1:9). Centuries before Whitman, the fertility cults of Asia Minor, with their phallic symbols, witnessed to the belief that the meaning of life is to be found in the worship of the processes of reproduction. The supreme act of worship was ritual fornication with the sacred prostitutes dedicated to the service of Eros. As an example, there were over a thousand "priestesses," or sacred courtesans, associated with the Temple of Aphrodite at Corinth.

There is a close and inseparable connection between idolatry and immorality, as St. Paul demonstrates in the opening chapter of the Epistle to the Romans. It is man's besetting sin to make idols. He tends, above everything else, to make an idol of sex. The awful thing

[19

about idols is their corruption of the mind and heart. "They that make them," says the Psalmist, "are like unto them" (Psalm 135:18). That is why the Apostle John writes: "Little children, keep yourselves from idols" (I John 5:21).

In "hipster" philosophy (the philosophy of the "Beat Generation") love is not the search for a mate, but (in Norman Mailer's expressive words) "the search for an orgasm more apocalyptic than the one which preceded it." "Hipster" love is nothing but the craving for detumescence, the experience of nervous discharge. In his mordant satire *Ape and Essence*, Aldous Huxley pillories the obsessive and orgiastic pursuit of orgasm. In a brilliant passage he describes a scene in the concert hall. A female baboon, "in shell pink evening gown, her mouth painted purple, her muzzle painted mauve, her fiery red eyes ringed with mascara," appears on the stage dragging behind her, "on all fours and secured by a light steel chain attached to a dog collar," Michael Faraday. She is about to sing when she catches sight of Faraday on his knees, in the act of straightening his bent and aching back. "Down, sir, down!" The tone is peremptory; she gives the old man a cut with her switch. Faraday winces and obeys; the audience laughs delightedly. She blows them a kiss, and then she sings the latest popular success:

> Love, Love, Love—
> Love's the very essence
> Of everything I think, of everything I do.
> Give me, Give me, Give me,

Give me detumescence
That means you.[10]

It is typical of Huxley's corrosive wit that he puts this philosophy into the mouth of an ape. ("Today, thanks to that Higher Ignorance, which is our knowledge, man's stature has increased to such an extent that the least among us is now a baboon, the greatest an orangutan or even, if he takes rank as a Saviour of Society, a true Gorilla.") Faraday, who belongs to a prehistoric age, is unutterably revolted by being forced to listen to this hysteric and lurid glorification of crude eroticism. His face "registers astonishment, disgust, indignation, and finally, such shame and anguish that tears begin to flow down the furrowed cheeks." He represents the natural man, uncorrupted and uncontaminated, before the final nuclear fall.

Today in our postwar society, there is an unhealthy and unclean preoccupation with sex. This accounts for the abnormal precocity of the average American child and the compulsive urge to sexual experimentation among teenagers. Modern advertising techniques are built, as Vance Packard has pointed out, upon the cynical and calculated exploitation of sex.[11] The advertising tycoons of Madison Avenue know that it is in the realm of sex that we are most vulnerable. They keep our sex instinct inflamed to make money out of us,

[10] New York: Harper & Row, Publishers, p. 36. Quoted by permission.
[11] *The Hidden Persuaders* (New York: David McKay Co., Inc., 1957). Also available in Pocket Book edition.

knowing that the man who has an obsession has little sales resistance.

Some say that sex is the surest and shortest way to happiness. They are cheats and liars. Happiness is never achieved by direct pursuit; as every philosopher knows, happiness can neither be bought nor manufactured. Happiness is always a by-product, life's free gift, and the man who seeks it directly is chasing a will-of-the-wisp. Happiness, like the pot of gold at the rainbow's end, will always evade and elude the man who makes it his chief goal or sole pursuit. It is not without interest that those who once pursued sex as the supreme experience are now turning to narcotics in a frantic search for bigger "kicks."

III. Sex and Contemporary Society

WHAT IS THE RELATION of the Christian understanding of sex to the mores and morals of our contemporary society? The Christian attitude toward sex is one of reverent responsibility. Christians do not joke about sex, William Temple said, for the same reason they do not joke about the sacrament of Holy Communion: it is not that sex is nasty, but that sex is sacred, and to joke about it is profanity.[12] Sex is a God-given gift to be kept

[12] *The Church Looks Forward* (New York: Macmillan Co., 1944), p. 77. Quoted by permission.

in trust for the beloved, that person to whom one is able to offer oneself in the glad and responsible union of lifelong marriage.

Petting

"Petting" (in campus vocabulary) is the exploitation of physical stimuli for the purposes of erotic pleasure. There is a legitimate place for pleasurable physical contact as a necessary part of preliminary love play; the objection to "petting" (as distinct from "necking") is that it involves the deliberate pursuit of sexual excitation, even to the point of orgasm, apart from and independently of the final act of intercourse. Christians believe that physical intercourse is properly reserved for the married estate. The objection to petting is that it deliberately initiates a sequence of events in separation from their natural end. Excessive sexual excitation, if denied its logical fulfillment, can only lead to increasing frustration and resentment.

Indulgence in the pursuit of passionate petting with extensive bodily contact may, of course, be associated with the preservation of actual virginity; but the question is whether the virginity thus preserved is anything other than technical. The editors of the volume, *Sex and the Church*, prepared by the Family Life Committee of the Lutheran Church-Missouri Synod, say:

The excuse that it avoids intercourse and preserves the girl's virginity is a moral subterfuge since the integrity of another person is violated . . . Petting cheapens sex . . . It often

[23

results in nervous tensions, feelings of indignity, resentfulness, hypocrisy. Petting experiences are stored in the conscious mind to plague and disturb. It is difficult to stop the demands for progressively increasing sex stimulation. Petting becomes a Frankenstein which the creator can no longer manage . . . Selfhood is exploited in heavy petting, and self-respect forfeited.[13]

Imagination and Self-Discipline

The Christian will feel the necessity to exercise in relation to premarital sexual activities that "self-control" and "self-discipline" which is the mark of the mature Christian, and which is required of the Christian in every department of life (cf. II Timothy 1:7).

For all young people the demands of sex are urgent and imperious. Nevertheless, the scriptural injunction is unambiguous: "Keep thyself pure" (I Timothy 5:22). A Christian will avoid what the moral theologian calls "occasions of sin": that is, situations in which one is exposed to special and unnecessary temptation. Christians will therefore question the wisdom of patronizing parking places for prolonged and protracted petting sessions. What is required is a realistic recognition of the dangers of invited temptation, and a sensible avoidance of excessive sexual stimulation.

It is an elementary psychological law that when the imagination and the will are in conflict, the imagination always wins. It is in the realm of the imagination that

[13] Oscar F. Feucht, ed., *Marriage and Family Research Series,* Volume 5 (St. Louis: Concordia Publishing House), p. 154. Quoted by permission.

the battle must be won. If the imagination is inflamed, the battle is already lost.

This fact provides us with a key by which to judge the efficacy of the methods which have been adopted by the military to fight venereal disease. Servicemen are not only instructed in the use of contraceptives, they are also issued them in their weekly pay packets. "The implication and suggestion is that the authorities expect a considerable number to practice fornication. There is no doubt," says William Temple, "that this method, by its inevitable suggestion, causes an increase of promiscuous intercourse, and therefore also an increase of the disease which it is designed to prevent. And the root trouble is the treatment of what is primarily a moral problem as if it were primarily a medical problem." [14] The concern of the military authorities is to make fornication medically safe. But if men were continent, there would be no medical problem. The problem is that what is primarily a moral problem with a medical aspect is treated as if it were primarily a medical problem with a moral aspect. The consequence of this basic confusion is to aggravate and make more difficult the problem of sexual morality. By the indiscriminate issue of contraceptives (to married and single alike), the imagination is inflamed, desire is aroused, and the will is weakened. The fact that a man has contraceptives (tactfully provided by the authorities) in his pay packet is sufficient, in itself, to set in operation the thought processes which, given the opportunity, will lead to acts of fornication. This is a shocking state

[14] *The Church Looks Forward*, p. 40.

[25

of affairs: a direct incentive to and encouragement of immorality.

Sex Education

Some educationalists are also culpable in this matter. In fact their moral guilt is greater because a pedagog ought to know better. According to *Harper's Magazine* [15] at least one college president admits that he would like "to make information on contraceptives part of the required freshman orientation lectures," but says that he does not dare to do so. The journalist (an M.D. on the staff of Cornell Medical College) points out that despite the fact that regulations existing in most colleges require that students of the opposite sex visiting each other's rooms must have, for example, "doors open, lights on, and four feet on the floor," sex relations do occur. He expresses the opinion that all students should know how to avoid the most serious consequences of immorality. Nevertheless, college officials admit that they are afraid of pressure from the Roman Church and Protestant fundamentalists; afraid of parents, alumni, and trustees; afraid that contributions from big business and conservative philanthropists or even state governments might stop—afraid of everything except the effect upon the sexual morality of students. There is, of course, a distinction between giving information in preparation for responsible living (and in the proper setting and at the appropriate time, contraceptive

[15] Milton I. Levine, M.D., and Maya Pines, "Sex: The Problem Colleges Evade," *Harper's Magazine* (October, 1961), pp. 129-132.

26]

knowledge), and giving instruction for the sole purpose of making sin "safe." The considerations weighing with today's typical college president are purely prudential. There could hardly be a more depressing example of moral neutralism and sinful irresponsibility.

Pornography

Christians have a special responsibility in relation to pornography—a startling substitution for the prudery that was a characteristic mark of the nineteenth century. Then there existed a conspiracy of silence and much hypocrisy: in the interests of modesty and of decency, it was customary to drape the legs of tables and of chairs. The facts of birth and reproduction were tactfully guarded from the minds of children, and the polite fiction was maintained that babies were found under gooseberry bushes. The objection to prudery, it has been said, is that it made "matters of sex secretive and unwholesome for the child, lustful for youth, and then resorted to face-saving moralisms." [16] Otto Piper observes: "Prudery, though it dares to speak of sexual matters only under the cloak of greatest secrecy, yet is no more devout or pure than unchastity, because it is not rooted in sexual respect, but in aversion to and fear of sex." [17] If Victorian prudery was carried to grotesque and extravagant lengths, the same accusation cannot be leveled against our contemporary society. We have

[16] *Sex and the Church*, p. 232.
[17] *The Biblical View of Sex and Marriage* (New York: Charles Scribner's Sons, 1960), p. 168. Quoted by permission.

lived to witness a dramatic reversal of attitudes, a sensational swing of the pendulum, in which prudery has been replaced by pornography. It is a question whether our last state is not worse than our first.

Pornography is the deliberate exploitation of the smutty and the salacious. Its proper emblem "should be a cock crowing on a dunghill, crowing not to greet the dawn but to salute the obscenity on which it has taken its stand." What we have today, this writer says, is "the deification of dirt, or the apotheosis of ordure." [18] Pornography seeks to arouse the indecent curiosity of the purient and the depraved by deliberately inciting and inflaming the imagination.

The aesthetes, in their dainty fashion, adopted the slogan "Art for Art's sake"—a slogan which enabled them to explore the dark paths of perversity. Under the convenient cloak of the pure love of literature, they were able to dabble in decadence and to justify, on the specious plea of the sovereignty of Art, their own preoccupation with vice. One is tempted to echo what John Wesley once said about a memorable debate in the House of Commons. The question before the House was the subject of slavery. The speaker admitted that slavery was an evil, but argued that it was "an evil interwoven with the most important interests of the country." To which Wesley made the fitting reply: "I deny that villainy is ever necessary."

The modern purveyors of pornography scorn such petty subterfuges and seductive slogans as Art for Art's

[18] Robert Elliot Fitch, *The Decline and Fall of Sex* (New York: Harcourt, Brace & World, Inc., 1951), p. 79. Quoted by permission.

sake: they wallow in filth, not for art's sake, but for obscenity's sake. It was Dostoievsky, that strange enigmatic Russian genius, who made the profound and penetrating observation that within the heart of every man there dwells both Sodom and the Madonna. Dostoievsky knew that within us all there are tragic schisms and latent contradictions. The writers of smut know our weakness and vulnerability: they know that lust, sadism, and depravity have the peculiar fascination of horror. And it is this fascination which the writers of pornography seek to exploit in a public, ostentatious parade of the outrageous and the obscene.

A clear distinction needs to be made between pornography and what is known as realist literature; it would appear that the basis of the distinction ought to be purpose and intention. Edward Wagenknecht in *Values in Literature* comments: "Simply because a work of art contains unpleasant material does not in the least mean that it is immoral in intent . . . In literary art subject matter is nothing. Treatment and attitude is everything." [19] Literature, as distinct from pornography, seeks to portray life, its muddy depths as well as its sublime heights. Its intended function is not to corrupt but to illuminate. By means of a sensitive and discriminating intelligence, the author of a work of literature seeks to bring to focus, in a clear and searching light, the vices and the virtues of men. Nevertheless, the fact that so many modern writers are preoccupied with sadism and seduction, lust and depravity, is in-

[19] Seattle: University of Washington Book Store, 1928, pp. 80-81. Copyright 1928, 1956 by Edward Wagenknecht.

[29

dicative of a moral sickness at the heart of contemporary society. One is tempted to expostulate, with King Lear: "There's hell, there's darkness, there is the sulphurous pit; burning, scalding, stench, consumption; fie, fie, fie! pah! pah!" [20]

IV. Sex and Marriage

EVERY THINKING person knows that something has gone wrong with sex as we know it. A disruption has taken place, and the consequence is disorder and confusion in the sexual lives of men and women. The Bible records with profound significance that the fall of mankind through disobedience and rebellion was accompanied, not only by the consciousness of guilt, but also by the awareness of nakedness, which became embarrassing after the entrance of sin. "The eyes of them both were opened, and they knew that they were naked; and they sewed fig leaves together and made themselves aprons" (Genesis 3:7). Interrogated by God, Adam confesses: "I heard thy voice in the garden,

[20] I would especially commend Edmund Fuller's incisive paperback *Man in Modern Fiction* (Vintage Books, 1949). He criticizes the false sentimentality which tends to glorify the depraved and the corrupt, and he scathingly denounces the clinical raw material and lubricious sexuality of much modern American writing.

and I was afraid, because I was naked; and I hid my-self." The experience of sin marks the end of innocence; in the realm of sexuality, it manifests itself in self-consciousness and shame.

No part of man's life is exempt from the evil entail of sin: man's sexual life, like his intellectual life and his religious life, is spoiled and soiled and subject to sin. It is necessary to stress, against those who would deify sex, that it is neither *less* corrupted than any other part of man's being, nor, against those who would make sex the fount and origin of all sin, is it *more* corrupted. Because of sin, sex, like every other part of man's being, needs redemption.

The Bible contains emphatic warnings against the abuse and misuse of sex. "Be not deceived," Paul writes to the citizens of the most notoriously profligate city of ancient antiquity. "Be not deceived: neither fornicators, nor idolaters, nor adulterers, nor effeminate, nor abusers of themselves with mankind . . . shall inherit the kingdom of God" (I Corinthians 6:9-10). The Christian ideal, it is clear, is continence before marriage and fidelity after marriage. "This is the will of God, even your santification, that ye should abstain from fornication" (I Thessalonians 4:3).

Sex Within Marriage

The liberty which the Christian man enjoys within marriage is not to be construed as legalized lust. St. Paul continues: "This is the will of God . . . that every one of you should know how to possess his vessel in

[31

sanctification and honour; not in the lust of concupiscence, even as the Gentiles which know not God"
(I Thessalonians 4:3-5). There is a healthy realism in
Paul: he knows that all men have not the gift of continence and that an enforced celibacy may hinder and
not help the achievement of sanctity, so that "it is better
to marry than to be aflame with passion" (I Corinthians
7:9, RSV). (It is not without interest that it is often
those who are most insistent on realism in literature
who take the most vigorous exception to the blunt
forthrightness of Paul's advice.) Marriage, he teaches,
is the divinely ordained prophylactic against sin. This
is not its sole purpose nor is it its main purpose, but it is
certainly one of its purposes. "To avoid fornication," he
adds, "let every man have his own wife, and let every
woman have her own husband. . . . Defraud ye not
one the other, except it be with consent for a time, that
ye may give yourselves to fasting and prayer; and come
together again, that Satan tempt you not for your in-
continency" (7:2-5).

What the Apostle enjoins on both husband and wife
is mutual consideration. What he urges is a deference
to, a sympathetic concern for, the desires and wishes of
the other. To our sophisticated ears, the residual lega-
tees of a democratic civilization, this advice may sound
trite and commonplace; it was startling and revolution-
ary advice to those to whom Paul wrote. The position
of women in the ancient world was one of real sub-
jection and social inferiority. A Jew thanked God daily
that he had not been created a Gentile, a slave, or a
woman. In Graeco-Roman society a woman was not a

companion but a chattel. Demosthenes cynically observed: "We have courtesans for the sake of pleasure; we have concubines for the sake of daily cohabitation; we have wives for the purpose of having children legitimately, and of having a faithful guardian for all our household affairs." The Greeks kept their wives in absolute seclusion (a married woman could never appear on the street alone and she could not have her meals in the apartments of the men), and at the same time, husbands sought their real pleasures in relationships outside of marriage.

Christianity was responsible for the inauguration of a new understanding of the role of a woman. "There is," Paul insists, "neither Jew nor Greek, there is neither bond nor free, there is neither male nor female: for ye are all one in Christ Jesus" (Galatians 3:28). In Christ all differences, racial, social, and sexual, are transcended. Nevertheless, the differences remain; they are not obliterated. We are "all one in Christ"; but there is still sexual differentiation, we remain both "male and female." What Christianity teaches is a new equality of status combined with a recognition that there is a difference of function. In the ancient world it was equality of status which needed to be stressed; today it is difference of function which needs to be reaffirmed. Some of the maladies and maladjustments from which our society suffers are due to the fact that men and women have rebelled against the natural distinctions of sex. It is regrettable that the ardent pursuit of equality by those who call themselves feminists has often been associated with an aggressive repudiation of femininity.

[33

In the inscrutable providence of God, a woman's unique privilege is that of motherhood, and a man's special responsibility is that of provider and protector. Nothing but confusion can result from ignoring these real distinctions, which are part and parcel of God's economy. It is still true that a woman achieves her true glory when she is most feminine.

Parenthood and Birth Control

Christians believe that those who enjoy the delights of marriage should also accept, with a sense of due responsibility, its disciplines. Parenthood is both a joy and a burden, a privilege and a responsibility. Christians will not selfishly seek to evade this inestimable privilege except for the most weighty reasons. "Not to rear up children," said Clement of Alexandria bluntly, "is to dissolve states and society and is an unmanly evasion of responsibility." It is easy to rationalize our repudiation of God's command on the ground of other responsibilities and pressing preoccupations. We all, in our selfishness and sin, reveal an astonishing ingenuity in finding good reasons for bad actions.

The question of the number of children whom a particular couple may plan to have is a matter to be determined before God in the light of time and circumstance. As John Donne pointed out in another connection, "no man is an island," and in this twentieth century, no responsible person can ignore the fact of the population explosion, and the increasing pressure on living space, and the limitation of available re-

34]

sources. In America and Australia the pressure is not yet acute; in India and Japan the situation is one of desperate seriousness. What might be responsible action in one place might well be criminal irresponsibility in another. No man lives unto himself.

In thinking about the question of the number of children they hope to have, a Christian couple will take into account their ability to meet the material demands of providing for and educating each successive child. For the achievement of healthy development, what is required is a home in which there is love and security. Christian parents know that emotional security is just as important as material security. This means that the relationship between husband and wife needs to be resilient, a happy relationship of genuine give and take. Marriage is meant to be a partnership and not a dictatorship.

It is a shocking thing when children are used as pawns, compelled to take sides in a relentless war of attrition between husband and wife. Nor should children be conceived in the expectation that they will solve existing tensions; they will not solve them, they will only reflect them. It is sometimes said that there are no problem children, but only problem parents. This is an exaggeration, but it contains some measure of truth. Humanly speaking, by our attitudes and example, we have it in our hands to make or mar. By understanding love, we can create an atmosphere which is encouraging and reassuring, or by our lack of understanding love, we can instill fear and insecurity. The procreation of children to boost one's own ego or to

[35

solve one's own problems is simply immoral; it often bears bitter fruit in implacable resentment and psychological rejection.

Each couple will decide for themselves the extent to which they avail themselves of contraceptive knowledge. It is difficult to see that any moral objection can be raised to the responsible use of contraceptives by married couples when the purpose is to plan and space children and to safeguard the health of the wife.

It is sometimes claimed that contraception is "unnatural." The question is what is "natural." Man is continually interrupting and changing the course of nature. His dignity lies in "subduing" it (in accordance with the biblical word, Genesis 1:28). He has it in his hands to shape and transform it; this is his duty and responsibility. The methods used by nature to limit the abundant fecundity of life have been, as the Reverend Thomas R. Malthus pointed out in 1798,[21] such positive checks as starvation, disease, and war. Today other methods, less dysgenic, are at the disposal of man.

The argument that contraception is "unnatural" would only be valid if it could be claimed that the sole justification for intercourse is conception. But this is plainly not so. Intercourse, as we have seen, is a means whereby a married couple enjoy and express love; it witnesses to the love which binds them, and it further strengthens that love. It is in the first place unitive, and it is also procreative. It can hardly be argued that the sole "natural" function of intercourse is procreation, be-

[21] *On Principles of Population as It Affects the Future Importance of Society.*

cause the days in the monthly menstrual cycle when conception is possible are comparatively few. No one would suggest that physical relations should cease with the onset of menopause: How then would a married couple, who in the normal course of events might justifiably expect to live together as man and wife for a further thirty years, express the biblical truth that they are "one flesh"? When St. Paul discusses the place of sexual intercourse in marriage, he discusses it, not from the point of view of reproduction, but as a mutual obligatory service which the spouses owe each other. The limits are set, significantly enough, not by the demands of procreation but by the mutual desires of the partners in relation to prayer and fasting (I Corinthians 7:3 ff).

The Roman Catholic Church is the most implacable opponent of "artificial" contraception. Yet the position adopted by the Roman Catholic Church is inconsistent and indefensible. Roman Catholic moral theologians, while affirming that the intended end of intercourse is procreation, nevertheless recognize the propriety of intercourse during what is termed the "safe period." Those who adopt this view admit that intercourse may properly be undertaken for purposes other than conception. Pope Pius XI, in the Bull *Casti Connubi* (1931), agrees that intercourse is lawful, even without any intention of children, providing no mechanical device is employed to prevent conception. A Roman Catholic couple, who feel conscientiously unable to have further children, are restricted to the use of "the safe period" or the rhythm method. The consequence is a gnawing feeling of uncertainty and a sense of anxious fear. (There is no absolute certainty about the exact limits of the "safe period" nor any guarantee that it is invariably safe.) Furthermore, the occasions of intercourse are necessarily limited to the particular period each month which is believed to be safe. This arbitrary restriction of intercourse to certain days militates against true spontaneity. The approved days may not coincide with either desire or convenience.

It is difficult to see what advantage there is in the use of a method which is uncertain in operation and limited in occasion over against the adoption of a method which is scientifically sound and incomparably more safe. On this matter each Christian couple will, finally, form their own judgment in the light of the "causes" for which marriage was instituted by God. Many Christians feel that the morality or immorality of contraception depends primarily, not upon the means or methods employed, but upon the ends which contraception is made to serve. The use of contraceptives by any person, whether married or unmarried, for the purposes of sexual promiscuity, is plainly wrong; the use of contraceptives by married people to escape and evade the responsibility of parenthood (except in cases of overriding necessity) is also wrong. The honored principle is *abusus non tollit usum*, abuse does not bar use. Many Christians believe there is a proper and legitimate place for the employment of contraceptives within marriage. As Bernard Shaw put it in his vivid epigrammatic way, "the difference between voluntary,

38]

rational, controlled activity and any sort of involuntary, irrational, and uncontrolled activity is the difference between an amoeba and a man."

Sex Outside of Marriage

There are, of course, manifold temptations to promiscuity. The availability of contraceptive knowledge has undoubtedly increased these temptations. In the Bible adultery is the term used to describe marital infidelity; fornication is the word used to describe sexual immorality before marriage. The Bible condemns both adultery and fornication. The Christian standard is chastity before marriage and fidelity after marriage.

The pursuit of indiscriminate sexual satisfaction always involves, to a greater or lesser extent, the sin of exploitation. The person who is intent on the mere enjoyment of sexual gratification is selfishly using another as a means to an end, and is treating a human being as a plaything and a toy. This is the degradation of love. Sexual intercourse becomes meaningful and significant only as the expression and reward of love. That is why prostitution is so degrading and corrupting: all the concomitants of love are absent. A woman who sells her body degrades herself; the implication is that she regards herself as a physical object and not as a person. Lecky, echoing Augustine, said of the prostitute: "herself the supreme type of vice, she is ultimately the most efficient guardian of virtue." This statement is morally fallacious and historically untrue. Virtue and vice are

[39

opposite sides of the one coin, and the man who begins by condoning and extenuating vice always ends by debasing and degrading virtue.

It is always difficult for the man who has been promiscuous to accept willingly the binding obligations of marriage. Kipling expresses the depressing testimony of experience when he writes:

> I've taken my fun where I've found it,
> An' now I must pay for my fun,
> For the more you 'ave known of the others
> The less you will settle to one.
>
> (*The Ladies*)

Thomas Jefferson, writing from Paris in 1785, criticized the sexual mores of the French nobility and noted: "conjugal love, having no existence among them, domestic happiness, of which that is the basis, is utterly unknown." He declared that the French were trapped in evil passions and pursuits "which offer moments of ecstasy, amidst days and months of restlessness and torment." He contrasted the situation in Europe with the "tranquil, permanent felicity with which domestic society in America blesses most of its inhabitants; leaving them to follow steadily those pursuits which health and reason approve, and rendering truly delicious the intervals of those pursuits." In a subsequent letter he pointed out that the man who develops a "passion for whores" (and this was the danger to which he believed an American seeking an education in Europe was exposed) "learns to consider fidelity to the marriage bed as an ungentlemanly prac-

40]

tice, and inconsistent with happiness." Jefferson was an acute and intelligent observer: he saw the consequences which inevitably follow in the realm of domestic happiness from the hedonistic pursuit of promiscuous pleasure.

Extramarital intercourse is always unsatisfactory. It lacks the sanctity of society and the element of public approval which attaches to marriage, and it lacks stability and security—an aspect that cannot be ignored if children are the fruit of the union. Extramarital intercourse is often a furtive and fleeting affair—the carnal consequence of impulse and passion. It is often a predatory and selfish thing. In any case, it lacks the quality of total self-giving which finds its fulfillment and expression in marriage.

V. The Nature of Love

THERE IS WIDESPREAD CONFUSION concerning the meaning and nature of love. It has been said that the word *love* can mean anything from Hollywood to Heaven. Probably no word has been so loosely bandied about, so prostituted and degraded, as the word *love*, and it is high time that it was rescued from the hands of the Philistines and, like the ark of old, brought back to Jerusalem.

[41

In the New Testament husbands are enjoined to "love" their wives as Christ loved the church (Ephesians 5:25). Christ's love for the church is shown in the fact that He died for it. The love (*agape*) which is to find expression in Christian marriage is to be of the same self-giving quality. It is to be unreserved and total, unswerving and faithful, sacrificial and self-denying. Such love (*agape*) needs to be differentiated from other forms of love: from *philia*, which expresses itself in companionship and mutual helpfulness, and *eros*, which commonly refers to physical desire. *Agape, philia* and *eros* are all to be found as constituents in Christian marriage. One writer makes the just observation: "without physical attraction, or *eros*, there would be no sexual union; without companionship, *philia*, there could be no life in common, or union of two whole personalities; and both of these are raised to a new level by the bond of a common faith and by self-giving devotion to each other (*agape*) out of commitment to Christ." [22] All elements must be present, in harmonious combination, for the achievement of Christian marriage.

Factors in Harmonious Marriage

In many circles there is a preoccupation with physical attraction to the neglect of such fundamental questions as temperamental compatability, intellectual suitability, and spiritual affinity. The presence of these other factors, so important from the point of view of marital harmony, can only be discovered from the ex-

[22] *Sex and the Church*, p. 224.

perience of shared activity. Certainly they cannot be discovered from the experience of watching, in silent passivity, a cinema show or a television screen. A couple who are attracted to one another will be conscious of a growing regard, compounded of admiration and affection; it is from this developing awareness of mutual regard and affection that friendship matures into love. It is safe to say that no lasting relationship of love is possible without a threefold experience of attraction, affection, and admiration. As friendship deepens and ripens into love, it becomes more and more exclusive. It is then possible to think in terms of formal engagement. An engagement is an acknowledgement of intent to marry and a declaration of honesty and good faith. It also allows a further period of preparation before the couple enter into the married estate: a period during which, with the greater freedom that is possible, a couple explore frankly matters which are of mutual interest and concern.

Among such matters are those of Christian witness and church affiliation. These questions need to be discussed and settled *before* marriage: too often a couple adopt the view that, because they love each other, love is all that matters and that every difficulty will solve itself. This confidence is touching, but unhappily unrealistic. There are many rocks on which the frail ship of matrimony can be wrecked. The wise mariner will anticipate, not invite, danger.

Each contentious question, as it arises, needs to be faced calmly and patiently and with honest realism. Christians are not exempt from the perplexities and

[43

problems which belong to our human situation. The question is in what spirit we confront our difficulties and meet our problems. In those matters in which there is legitimate difference of opinion, Christians will seek to achieve a common mind by reflection and prayer. Christians in their relationship with one another will seek to observe the divine law of Charity, remembering that:

Charity suffereth long, and is kind; charity envieth not; charity vaunteth not itself, is not puffed up,
Doth not behave itself unseemly, seeketh not her own, is not easily provoked, thinketh no evil;
Rejoiceth not in iniquity, but rejoiceth in the truth;
Beareth all things, believeth all things, hopeth all things, endureth all things.

(I Corinthians 13:4-7)

As Robert Elliot Fitch puts it, love is "commingled with courage, tempered by duty, proved by suffering, sweetened with tenderness, made strong in faithfulness." [23]

Sex and the Kinsey Report

The chaotic state of present-day sexual morality is sufficiently indicated by the statistical evidence collated and analyzed by Dr. Kinsey. Dr. Kinsey demonstrates that there is widespread sexual lawlessness. He confirms the truth of what informed people have for a long time either known or suspected. It is not necessary

[23] *The Decline and Fall of Sex,* p. 75.

to challenge the general accuracy of the statistical picture which he presents; but it is entirely proper to question Dr. Kinsey's presuppositions and assumptions.

The late Dr. Kinsey was a professional zoologist: he applies to the study of the human male and female (it is significant that he deliberately chooses to use these "biologic" terms) the statistical methods which he used so successfully in the study of gall wasps. He cannot see, however, that sexuality in man is something different from sexuality in animals, and that for human beings, there is a fundamental distinction between what a man can do and what he ought to do. Dr. Kinsey disclaims the role of a moralist: he is, he insists, a scientist and nothing more. In an early work entitled *Methods in Biology* Kinsey praises the teacher "who treasures the varieties of observed data as against all authors, ancient and modern, and against fashion, creed, convention and cult." Nevertheless, as Geoffrey Gorer points out, "behind the mask of dispassionateness, you can easily discern Dr. Kinsey's astonished admiration for the people with the larger rates of 'outlet' and his contemptuous pity for those making poor scores." He continues: "a little anthropological knowledge might have rectified this attitude. We have information from enough primitive societies to suggest that there is an (apparently) direct correlation between high rates of intercourse and lack of emotional interest in sex or belief in love." He rightly reminds us that "for a society that believes in love, be it sacred or profane, the physiological aspect of love cannot be separated from the emotional and psychological con-

[45

comitants without reducing it to meaninglessness." [24]

No one can read the Report without noting Dr. Kinsey's inferences concerning "normal" sexual behavior. He suggests that sex may be interpreted as "a normal biologic function, acceptable in whatever form it is manifested." [25] He admits, however, that by "English and American standards" this view is considered "primitive, materialistic or animalistic, and beneath the dignity of a civilized and educated people." The question which we must ask is this: Is "normal" behavior to be interpreted as the statistical average, or is it to be interpreted as that which is in harmony with the true nature of man as a self-determining and morally responsible human being? Again and again Dr. Kinsey makes pejorative judgments about traditional morality: he equates what is "average" with what is "normal" and implies what is "normal" is what is "right." Dr. Kinsey continues to affirm that it is the "biologic" which should determine moral conduct and behavior.

We are not concerned to dispute Dr. Kinsey's statistical percentages nor his graphs of sexual activity; what we are concerned to dispute is Dr. Kinsey's behavioristic conclusions in the realm of sexual morality. Millicent McIntosh, in a symposium which seeks to analyze and evaluate the findings of Dr. Kinsey, says that "the Kinsey Report uses all the techniques to which Americans are especially vulnerable. Its pages and pages of statistics, while dull and very depressing, are equally

[24] *The American Scholar,* Summer 1948. Quoted by permission.
[25] *The Sexual Behavior of the Human Male* (Philadelphia: W. B. Saunders Company, 1948), p. 263. Quoted by permission.

impressive to the ordinary person." She points out how easily a person's defenses can be broken down by the unscrupulous manipulation of these statistics.

All boys and girls are pathetically anxious to be 'normal' . . . They are especially vulnerable in the whole area of boy-girl relationships. Whatever is done by the crowd is what they must do, lest they risk being peculiar, blue stocking, prudish, with the inevitable result of unpopularity. So if the Kinsey Report announces that ninety one percent of females have done petting by the age of twenty five, and eighty one percent by the age of eighteen, the girl who is being pressed by a boy to go further than she thinks proper feels herself trapped by these statistics. If she is not erotically aroused, or does not wish to be, she begins to wonder if she is normal.[26]

The problem arises from the acceptance of the unspoken but implied assumption that what everyone does we may do, indeed ought to do. A university counselor stated that many college boys felt that they were not actually virile if they could not keep up with the statistics Dr. Kinsey presents of sex experience for males of their age. The consequence is that the relative standards of men are progressively substituted for the absolute standards of God.

Sex and the Christian

The Christian recognizes that he is neither angel nor animal, neither pure spirit nor pure body, but a body-

[26] *An Analysis of the Kinsey Reports on Sexual Behavior in the Human Male and Female,* edited by Donald Porter Geddes (New York: E. P. Dutton and Company, Inc., 1954), pp. 139-140. Quoted by permission.

[47

soul dualism, and that sex is a good gift of God, both mysterious and holy. Today the mystery of sex has been largely lost in a preoccupation with diagrammatic detail. But Christian love is something far more profound than the knowledge of anatomy and questions of technique: it is both physical and spiritual, a meeting and a mingling of two persons in a mutuality of self-giving love. What is required for a full understanding of love is a rediscovery of the sanctity of sex, its mysterious beauty and sacramental holiness. Significantly, it is often those who boast most loudly about their sexual ability who fail most miserably in the testing situation of marriage, in the achievement of a satisfactory and satisfying sex relationship.

If sex is to regain its healthy and wholesome character, it must be given again its private and intensely personal character. Reinhold Niebuhr comments: "A sophisticated effort to destroy modesty and a sense of shame by the simple device of making the function of sex more public is bound to aggravate rather than alleviate the difficulties of a man's sex life." [27] Augustine describes the attempt which the Cynics made to strip sex of its veil: "It was," he writes, "against the modesty of natural shame that the Cynic philosophers struggled so hard in the error of their astonishing shamelessness; they thought that intercourse between husband and wife was indeed honorable and that therefore, it should be done in public. Such barefaced obscenity deserved to receive a doggish name, so they went by the title of

[27] *The Nature and Destiny of Man,* Volume I (New York: Charles Scribner's Sons, 1941), p. 239. Quoted by permission.

Cynics" (a designation which means doglike). The ancients understood the true character of the Cynic philosophy, and they called it by its proper name.

VI. Problems Relating to Sex

THIS PLEA FOR SEXUAL MODESTY, for an attitude of reverence and a sense of reticence, is not to be construed as a justification for ignoring or evading the facts of sex. Ignorance in this field is *not* bliss. There are great and grievous dangers in ignorance. The child who is deprived of sexual knowledge is handicapped for the battle of life. The child who is forewarned is forearmed, therefore the better able to meet the disturbing demands and resist the temptations of puberty and maturing sexuality.

Sexual Crimes

Sexual crimes, as every criminologist knows, are often the consequence of blind and ignorant experimentation. A crime is often the brutal work of a baffled creature, groping and desperately wanting to know. Otto Piper writes: "Young people easily fall victim to desperate methods in their search for the answer to the mystery. . . ." They may start "reading obscene literature, and associating with prostitutes. The great number of suicides in the seventeen-to-twenty-one-year-old bracket is another tragic commentary on the disastrous result of this consuming perplexity." [28]

There are additional reasons for wise instruction. In our fallen society, there are always wicked men eager and ready to take advantage of the "innocent abroad." Parents who fail to answer, frankly and honestly, the questions of their growing children, and who fail to impart information according to the children's capacity to receive it, are guilty of moral abdication. Sex is both mysterious and beautiful, and it can easily be desecrated and made smutty and unclean by those who are defiled and unbelieving, to whom nothing is pure (Titus 1:15). It was Havelock Ellis, that pioneer of sex education, who said that withholding the best sex instruction is like refusing to supply pure water because there are puddles in the street to drink from. It needs to be stressed that sex education is best given by parents within the home, and only in the second place, by educators, pastors, and doctors.

Sexual Temptation

A word needs to be said about sexual temptation. We cannot help temptations coming into the mind; the question is whether, when they come, they are lustfully welcomed or summarily rejected and repelled. "I may not be able to stop the birds flying over my head,"

[28] *The Biblical View of Sex and Marriage*, p. 42.

Luther commented in his down-to-earth fashion, "but I can stop them from nesting in my hair." Nature abhors a vacuum. If we desire to avoid evil thoughts, then we must fill our minds with good thoughts. Thomas Chalmers spoke of "the expulsive power of a new and a nobler affection": he meant that if we would expel impure and ignoble thoughts, we must occupy ourselves with those thoughts which are honest, just, pure, lovely, and of good report (Philippians 4:8).

According to the book of Proverbs, as a man thinks in his heart, so he is (23:7). In biblical psychology, the heart stands for the center of a man's thinking and being. We still speak colloquially of what a man is "at heart." Jesus pointed out that our habitual thoughts are a key to the inclinations of our heart and determine the kind of person we are. "For out of the heart proceed evil thoughts, murders, adulteries, fornications . . ." (Matthew 15:19). The thought, as a popular proverb puts it, is father of the deed. That is why Jesus said "that whosoever looketh on a woman to lust after her hath committed adultery with her already in his heart" (Matthew 5:28). Jesus was not speaking of normal sexual desires: He was speaking of lascivious and lustful and forbidden thoughts (cf. II Samuel 11:2). He was speaking of the man who uses his eyes to awaken his lust, who looks lasciviously so that passion is awakened and desire is aroused. The Apostle Peter refers to those who have "eyes full of adultery" (II Peter 2:14). He is speaking of those whose minds are defiled and whose thoughts are depraved. To the pure all things are pure, but to the man whose heart is defiled every

[51

woman is an object of indecent and impure and improper interest. "Man," as Acquinas said, "sees the deed but God sees the intention": that is why it is only the pure in heart who see God and who are blessed of God (Matthew 5:8).

Celibacy

Marriage is God's destiny for most men. Only the most weighty and compelling reasons should lead a man to repudiate this destiny. To advocate celibacy, in contradiction to the divine decree (Genesis 1:28), is bluntly designated "a doctrine of devils" (I Timothy 4:1-3). "Since sex is indispensable to God's plan for service," says Otto Piper, "only the most compelling reasons, in accordance with His redemptive purposes, can release a person from the duty to marry. No one may act arbitrarily in this matter." [29] The person who rejects the vocation of marriage, except in response to a call of God for some particular task, deprives himself of immeasurable grace and strength, and exposes himself to manifold temptations. The biblical principle has a wide application: he that seeketh his life will lose it, but he that loseth his life will find it (Matthew 16:25).

The situation in regard to involuntary celibacy is different. The single woman who, through no fault of her own, finds herself deprived of the inestimable blessing of marriage, needs special sympathy and support. Certainly nothing can excuse the cruel gibes about "old maids" which are often thoughtlessly and heartlessly made. Such persons are the special object

[29] *The Biblical View of Sex and Marriage,* p. 107.

of God's care and concern, and many of them testify gladly that the valley of Achor has become a door of hope and a means of blessing (Hosea 2:15).

Sterility

We turn to a consideration of a number of other particular problems. It is generally known that sterility is increasing in incidence. The question is whether, when the problem is the infertility of the husband, the couple should think in terms of artificial insemination. This is a subject which needs the most careful thought. So often we fail to base practice on principle; the result, of course, is moral chaos and confusion. It is usual to make a distinction between A. I. H. (artificial insemination from the husband) and A. I. D. (artificial insemination from a donor). A. I. H. is possible when the problem is physiological and not biological. The morality of A. I. H. is not in question; the morality of A. I. D. is a matter of continuing debate. There would seem to be two basic questions: whether any man, as donor, has the right to engage in anonymous parenthood (that is, whether any man has the moral right to sire offspring, the identity of which he will never know, and for whom he can accept no responsibility); and secondly, whether any woman, having pledged absolute loyalty and fidelity to her husband, is morally justified in seeking artificial insemination from an unknown donor.

The Eastern Church describes adultery as the "death" of marriage, because it destroys, in a way which other sins do not, the physical reality which is symbolized by the phrase "one flesh." Adultery invades

[53

the very sanctum of marriage, and it is clear that adultery, if persisted in, will eventually kill a marriage. The question is whether or not A. I. D. destroys the sacred sanctity of the marriage contract. A number of conscientious and mature couples believe that it does not. On the other hand, a Canadian judge has ruled that A. I. D. is *legally* indistinguishable from adultery, and English courts have ruled that artificially inseminated children are illegitimate. The fact that a husband acquiesces or even approves has no bearing on the moral and legal issues involved; if a thing is wrong, it cannot be made right by the mere whim of the parties concerned. Interestingly, a leading American psychiatrist, who finds unconscionable any likening of A. I. D. to adultery, mentioned recently that the unconscious of couples who have arranged for A. I. D.—the woman's more than the man's—is often in agreement with that of the courts, i.e., "*irrationally* they may experience the event as something very much akin to . . . adultery."

In the marriage service, a couple take each other "for better, for worse, for richer, for poorer, in sickness and in health." This vow may be regarded as including the patient acceptance of such hazards and hardships as involuntary sterility. Childlessness is not the supreme deprivation, and there is always the possibility of adoption.

Homosexuality

The problem of homosexuality is one of exceptional difficulty. Homosexuality is often a passing phase of

54]

early adolescence. What is required in relation to homosexual experimentation or practice is genuine repentance and the scrupulous avoidance of further temptation. It is specious rationalization to argue that homosexuality is innate, normal, "natural"; it may, indeed, be the expression of sexual immaturity or a serious personality maladjustment, but it is plainly not in accordance with the biological ends of "nature." Paul makes it clear, in the opening chapter of the Epistle to the Romans, that homosexuality is a denial of God's intention in creation because it involves changing "the natural use into that which is against nature."

Homosexuals often like to believe that their homosexuality is inborn, therefore irremediable. Such indeed was the theory propounded approximately a century ago; it is still widely held by the uninformed and the misinformed. Today, however, the concept of homosexuality as constitutional (in the sense of genes and chromosomes) in etiology is considered by leading scientific investigators largely as obsolete. Most psychiatrists regard the disorder as essentially acquired—the result of psychological rather than physical disturbances. Among these medical authorities, some would admit constitutional factors (such as aspects of temperament, energy, and body build) as *predisposing* to the establishment of a homosexual pattern of sexual behavior, but not in a one-to-one causation; they believe such constitutional factors interact with psychological and social factors in a complex and varied pattern that differs from case to case.

Freud assumed a bisexual start in every individual,

[55

with relationships to parents, nurses, teachers, early companions, and a wide range of additional factors determining the ultimate development: normal sexuality, homosexuality, or perversion. Homosexuality he concluded (as do psychiatrists today) to be an arrested stage of psychosexual development. Interested readers may find many references in psychoanalytic literature concerning the mental mechanisms and different life situations which may lead to homosexuality in men and women.

Whatever the cause (and no single one explains the aberration), it is important to realize that the condition is not one any individual should accept as hopeless. The overt homosexual, or the person with homosexual inclinations, needs to regard his *illness* as such and to seek qualified treatment for it in psychotherapy, which offers the greatest hope of lasting cure. If the homosexual wants help, he or she can get it; and in the great majority of cases, that help can be effective.

It is now widely felt that, while the practice of homosexuality is rightly a matter for moral condemnation, it is not a proper matter for legal prosecution, except in cases involving the seduction and corruption of minors and offences against public decency. At this point the law appears to be inconsistent in its attitude and arbitrary in its application. Neither the woman who in private practices female homosexuality (lesbianism), nor the person who indulges in adultery, is liable to legal prosecution; but the man who indulges in homosexuality is exposed to the most severe and stringent penalties

56]

of the law. What the Christian must believe and say is that every kind of sexual immorality is wrong and therefore sinful. Whether offences that are sins in the eyes of God (and therefore subject to His wrath) should also be crimes in the eyes of the law (and therefore subject to civil punishment) is a matter requiring the most careful examination. Whatever conclusion is reached on this controversial question, it still remains true that there is no moral justification for the perpetuation of a double standard.

Masturbation

Masturbation is not a subject about which the Bible speaks. (The sin of Onan [Genesis 38:8 ff], which is often interpreted as masturbation, was, in fact, *coitus interruptus*. In defiance of his duty towards his deceased brother, as required by Levirate law [Deuteronomy 25:5], Onan's selfish act deprived his deceased brother's wife of the possibility of begetting and bearing a child.) Masturbation is generally a passing phase; if the practice becomes compulsive and obsessive, it undoubtedly indicates some emotional maladjustment or psychological immaturity. It is generally accompanied by feelings of abject shame, guilt, and utter unworthiness. A form of adolescent self-love, it is essentially selfish and uncreative; and it needs to be replaced, in the ordinary course of events, by happy and healthy activity of an outgoing kind in mixed society.

[57

VII. Summary: The Christian's View

THE CHRISTIAN BELIEVES that sex, like God's other good gifts, ought to be "received with thanksgiving by those who believe and know the truth" (I Timothy 4:3). "It is precious because man's sexuality may be the means to highest fulfilment," says Norman Pittenger wisely, "but it can also be the means to lowest degradation: 'the higher we can rise, the lower we may fall.' The perverted sexuality of sinful man illustrates the truth: *corruptio optimi pessima*. The best, when it is corrupted, becomes the worst." [30] The Christian is aware that, in this sphere as in all others, he needs to know and experience God's forgiving love and transforming grace.

The sanctity of sex and the honorable estate of marriage are sufficiently indicated by the fact that God uses this relationship as an analogy to describe His own relationship with His people. In the book of Revelation, heaven is referred to as an everlasting marriage celebration, and the Second Coming of Christ is spoken

[30] *The Christian View of Sexual Behavior* (Greenwich, Conn.: The Seabury Press, Inc., 1954), p. 61. Quoted by permission.

of as a bridegroom coming to claim his bride. And the high esteem in which Jesus held marriage is shown by the fact that, in the days of His earthly ministry, He not only adorned and beautified the wedding at Cana with His presence, but made it the scene of His first recorded miracle.

Chastity is a badge of the Christian man and woman. Christians are not called to uncleanness but to holiness. They are to treat sex as sacred and marriage as honorable; they are to cultivate purity in thought and modesty in life. The proper use of sex is part of the Christian's grateful response to God, who made sex in creation, redeemed sex as part of the total person, and sanctified the proper use of sex through the Holy Spirit.[31]

[31] *Sex and the Church,* p. 234.